EXPLORING CONTINENTS

AFRICA

Deborah Underwood

Heinemann Library
Chicago, Illinois

Picture research by Mica Brancic
Design by Richard Parker and Q2A
Illustrations by Jeff Edwards

Library of Congress Cataloging-in-Publication Data

Underwood, Deborah

Africa / Deborah Underwood
p. cm. -- (Exploring continents)
Includes bibliographical data and indes.
ISBN 1-4034-8241-1 (library binding - hardcover) -- ISBN 1-4034-8249-7 (pbk.)

A full catalog record for this book is held at the Library of Congress.

Printed and bound in China by WKT

11 10 09 08 07
10 9 8 7 6 5 4 3 2 1

Acknowledgments

Picture acknowledgments: Corbis pp. **16** (Joe McDonald), **21** (Bettmann), **22** (SIME); Getty pp. **5** (National Geographic), **7** (Stone), **8** (Photographer's Choice), **9** (Photonica), **11** (Photographer's Choice), **12** (Photographer's Choice), **13** (Gallo Images), **14** (Taxi/Anup Shah), **15** (Image Bank), **18** Science Photo Library/Sam Ogden, **19** (Image Bank), **24** (Image Bank), **23** Network Photographers, **25** (Image Bank), **27**.

Cover satellite image of Africa reproduced with permission of SPL/M-Sat Ltd.

Every effort has been made to contact copyright holders of any material reproduced in this book. Any omissions will be rectified in subsequent printings if notice is given to the publisher.

CONTENTS

Words that appear in the text in bold, **like this**, are explained in the Glossary.

WHAT IS A CONTINENT?

Land on Earth is divided into seven large areas. These areas of land are called continents. Continents are the largest units of land on Earth. The continents are named Africa, Antarctica, Asia, Australia, Europe, North America, and South America.

Millions of years ago, the continents were all joined together. They formed a huge **landmass** named Pangaea. Over time, Earth's **crust** shifted. The landmass broke into pieces. These pieces slowly drifted apart and became the continents we know today.

This map shows the world's seven continents.

Did you know?

On most maps, the continents can look bigger or smaller than they really are. While North America and Africa may look about the same size, Africa is more than 2 million square miles (5.2 million square kilometers) larger than North America!

The Continent of Africa

Africa is the world's second largest continent, after Asia. Asia and Africa are connected by a small piece of land named the Sinai **Peninsula**. Oceans and seas surround Africa. The Atlantic Ocean laps at its west coast. The Mediterranean Sea and Red Sea can be found off its northern coasts. Africa's east coast meets the Indian Ocean.

Africa includes a number of islands. Madagascar lies off Africa's southeast coast. At 228,821 square miles (592,800 square kilometers), Madagascar is almost the size of California and Florida put together.

HOW BIG IS AFRICA?

- *Land area:* 11,720,000 square miles (30,365,000 square kilometers)
- *Distance north to south:* 5,000 miles (8,000 kilometers)
- *Distance east to west:* 4,700 miles (7,500 kilometers) at widest point

Africa is famous for its vast areas of grassland and fascinating wildlife.

WHAT DOES AFRICA LOOK LIKE?

Africa has many types of landscapes. They include vast deserts, sweeping **savannas**, and lush rain forests. East Africa has lots of mountains and lakes. Woodlands and grassy plains cover much of Africa's center.

High and Low

Most of Africa is made up of **plateaus**. These plateaus are large, high, and mostly flat. The highest plateaus are in the east and south. This area is called High Africa. Most of High Africa is more than 3,000 feet (910 meters) above sea level. The rest of the country makes up Low Africa. Low Africa ranges from 500 to 2,000 feet (150 to 610 meters) above sea level.

This map shows the main landscape features of Africa.

Africa's Great Rift Valley is about 4,000 miles (6,400 kilometers) long, and up to 60 miles (100 kilometers) wide.

Mountains

Africa does not have many mountain ranges. The Atlas Mountains are in northern Africa. The Ethiopian Highlands are to the east and the Drakensberg Range sits near the southern tip of the continent. The Ruwenzori Mountains can be found along the Great Rift Valley.

The highest peaks in Africa do not belong to mountain ranges. Mount Kilimanjaro and Mount Kenya are the tallest mountains in Africa. Both are **extinct** volcanoes. They rise out of the Great Rift Valley.

7

Deserts

The Sahara Desert stretches across northern Africa and is the largest desert in the world. Sand dunes cover about 25 percent of the Sahara. The rest of the desert is made of rocks and gravel.

The long Namib Desert hugs Africa's southwestern coast. It is 1,200 miles (1,900 kilometers) long, but only 80 to 100 miles (130 to 160 kilometers) wide. The northern Namib is made of gravel plains. The south is brick-red sands.

The Kalahari Desert in southern Africa is connected to the Namib and is mostly covered in sand. White **salt pans** shimmer in the north where a huge lake stood thousands of years ago. When the climate changed and the lake dried up, only the salts from its water remained.

Sand dunes in the Sahara Desert can stretch for miles.

Did you know?

Millions of years ago, animals gathered at lakes in the Great Rift Valley. When they died, layers of soil and ash from erupting volcanoes buried their bones. As Earth's crust shifted, the bones were brought back up to the surface. Many important **fossils** have been discovered here.

Lakes and Rivers

Africa's largest lakes can be found in the Great Rift Valley. Lake Victoria is the world's second-largest freshwater lake. It is more than three times the size of the state of West Virginia. Nearby Lake Tanganyika is the second-deepest lake in the world.

Africa is also home to the world's longest river. The Nile River flows north from Lake Victoria, and empties into the Mediterranean Sea. The Niger, Congo, and Zambezi are other major African rivers.

AFRICA LANDSCAPE FACTS:

- *Tallest mountain:* Mount Kilimanjaro 19,340 feet (5,895 meters)

- *Largest desert:* Sahara 3,320,000 square miles (8,600,000 square kilometers)

- *Longest river:* Nile 4,160 miles (6,695 kilometers)

- *Largest lake:* Lake Victoria 26,828 square miles (69,484 square kilometers)

The Zambezi River pours over a steep cliff to form the famous Victoria Falls. The Falls lie on the **border** between Zambia and Zimbabwe.

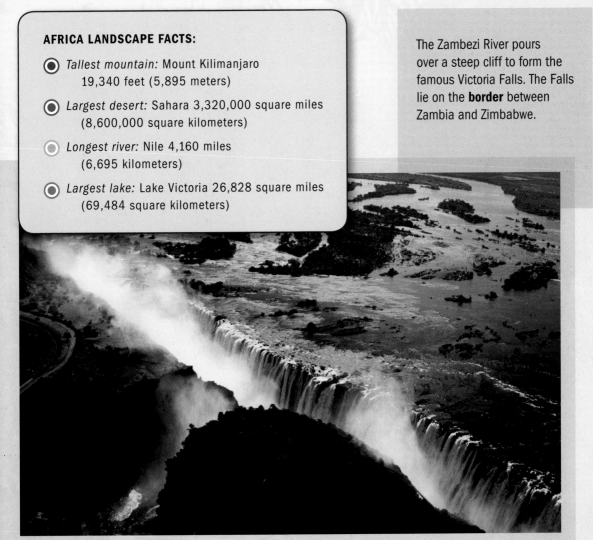

WHAT IS AFRICA'S CLIMATE LIKE?

The **equator** cuts through the middle of the continent, so Africa's climate is mostly warm or hot. However temperatures become lower at high **altitudes**. This means weather in Africa's mountain areas can be cold. Even though Mount Kilimanjaro is near the equator, its peak is capped with ice all year long.

Most of Africa falls into four major climate zones. From driest to wettest, the zones are **arid**, semi-arid, tropical dry, and tropical wet.

Africa's arid places are its deserts. Most of these areas receive less than 10 inches (250 mm) of rain per year. Daytime temperatures can be higher than 105°F (41°C), while night temperatures may drop below 32°F (0°C).

Atlas Mountains

Sahara Desert

Ethiopian Highlands

Equator

Congo Basin

Indian Ocean

N
W E
S

Atlantic Ocean

Namib Desert

Kalahari Desert

Rain forest
Temperate forest
Evergreen trees and shrubs
Grassland and savanna
Oasis and Nile valley
Semi desert (semi-arid zone)
Desert (arid zone)

0   800 miles
0   1000 km

This map shows the many different kinds of plants that live across the continent of Africa.

Semi-arid zones separate Africa's deserts from tropical areas. Semi-arid regions usually get 10 to 20 inches (250 to 510 mm) of rain per year. Temperatures range from below 32°F (0°C) to more than 100°F (38°C).

Tropical dry places have at least one wet season every year when much of their rain falls. Annual rainfall ranges from 20 to 60 inches (510 to 1,520 mm). Temperatures are hot all year. In some places, daily high temperatures average more than 90°F (32°C).

Africa's tropical wet areas are near the equator. They get lots of rainfall and are always hot, with average temperatures of more than 81°F (27°C). Some places receive more than 150 inches (3,810 mm) of rain per year. Rain falls all year, but is heavier in some months than in others.

The wettest rain forest areas can get more than 400 inches (10,160 mm) of rain per year.

HIGHS AND LOWS:

- Africa's highest recorded temperature was 136°F (58°C) at Al Aziziyah, Libya in 1922.

- Buffelsfontein in South Africa reached a lowest temperature of 0°F (-18°C) in 2005.

13

WHAT PLANTS AND ANIMALS LIVE IN AFRICA?

Because Africa has many different climates and landscapes, a wide range of plants and animals can live there. Some can be found all over the continent. Others live only in certain areas.

Date palms, fig trees, and shrubs are among the plants that might be found growing in an oasis.

Plant Life

Many plants have ways to survive the fierce heat and dry air of African deserts. Some have roots that reach more than 130 feet (40 meters) into the earth to find hidden water. Others store water for later use.

An island of green in a desert marks the presence of an **oasis**. In these spots, underground water comes near the surface.

In central Africa's rain forests, plants get plenty of water. Rain forests have a great variety of plant life, including mahogany trees, orchids, and African violets.

Desert Animals

Deserts may look empty, but they are full of life. Scarab beetles scuttle across sands. Slithering snakes hunt for rodents. Desert hedgehogs peek out from underground burrows. More than 300 types of birds spend some time each year in the Sahara.

Like desert plants, desert animals have ways to survive the hot, dry climate. Camels can go many days without drinking. Scorpions hide in the desert sand while the sun is out. Tiny fennec foxes have large ears that let heat escape from their bodies quickly.

Cobras can be found living in extremely dry conditions.

On the Savanna

Many types of animals make their homes on Africa's grassy plains and woodlands. During the dry season, some of these animals move closer to water holes to find the most tender plants. When rains come, the animals spread out again.

Giraffes are some of Africa's most recognizable animals. Their long necks allow them to eat tasty leaves high in the trees. The only other large animals on the savanna who can reach high leaves are elephants.

Giraffes use their long tongue to reach the leaves they eat.

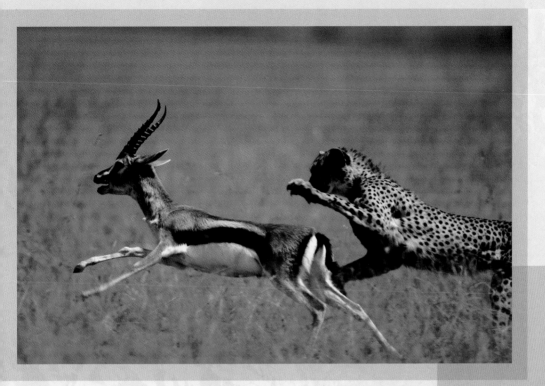

A cheetah closes in on a Thompson's gazelle.

Dozens of types of **antelopes** roam the savannas. Elands, duikers, impalas, nyalas, wildebeest, and dikdiks are all types of antelope. They vary greatly in size. An eland can weigh more than 10 people put together. The tiny dik-dik weighs only 10 to 12 pounds (4.5 to 5.5 kilograms)—about as much as a pet cat!

Africa's **carnivores** eat other animals. They rely on bursts of speed to catch their prey. Cheetahs can reach top speeds of 70 miles (113 kilometers) per hour! Other African carnivores include lions, wild dogs, and spotted hyenas.

Did you know?

Every year in East Africa, more than one million wildebeest, zebras, and gazelles begin their annual **migration**. They leave dry areas and move in a circular path looking for fresh grasses to eat. They travel more than 800 miles (1,287 kilometers) a year.

Rain Forest Creatures

Many of Africa's rain forest animals are found nowhere else on Earth. The rare pygmy hippopotamus lives near swamps and rivers. It measures only about 5 feet (1.5 meters) long. The okapi looks like a zebra, but it is really related to the giraffe. It has a rich brown coat, with white stripes on its legs. Chimpanzees live in Africa's rain forests and woodlands. Gorillas live in rain forests and mountain areas near the equator.

The fates of Africa's plants and animals are tied together. Forests shrink as people cut down trees to get wood or to clear land for crops. Chimpanzees, gorillas, and others who dwell in these forests are losing their homes.

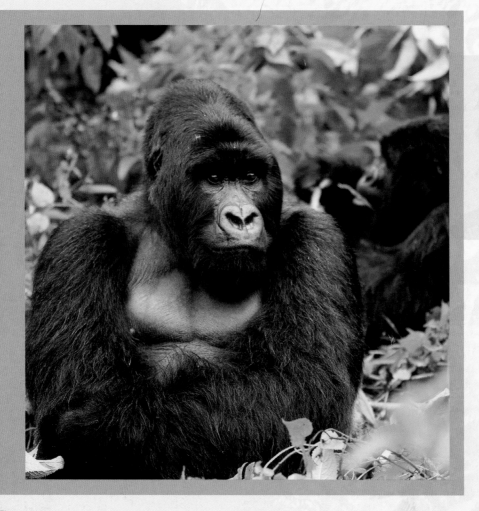

If the African forests are not saved, animals, such as these gorillas, will vanish from the wild forever.

WHAT ARE AFRICA'S NATURAL RESOURCES?

Africa is rich in natural resources. Diamonds, gold, and oil are just a few of the resources hidden deep in Africa's soil. The most valuable **minerals** come from a small handful of countries.

Most of Africa's oil comes from two areas: north Africa, and the west coast of central Africa. The country of Nigeria produces the most oil. Libya, Algeria, Angola, and Egypt are other major producers.

Crops
- Cacao
- Coffee
- Cotton
- Fruit
- Maize
- Millet
- Sugar
- Tea
- Wheat

Mining
- Minerals and ores

Power
- Coal
- Gas
- Oil

Industry
- Fishing
- Forestry

Livestock
- Cattle
- Sheep

Indian Ocean

Atlantic Ocean

| 0 | 800 miles |
| 0 | 1000 km |

This map shows where Africa's natural resources and main crops can be found.

Mineral Wealth

Many precious metals and gems are mined in Africa. The country of South Africa produces more gold than any other country in the world. Around half of the world's diamonds come from Africa. Botswana mines more diamonds than any other African country.

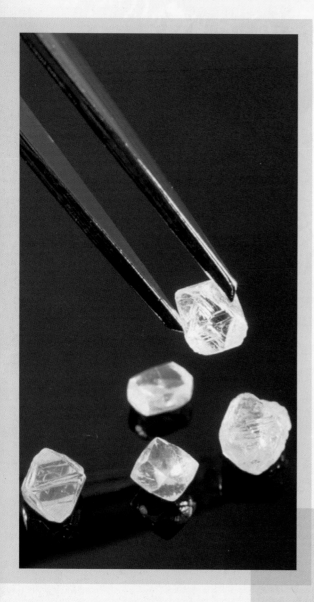

Africa produces many other minerals, too. Guinea has over one-third of the world's **reserves** of bauxite, which is used to make aluminum. A large share of the world's phosphate reserves are in Morocco. Phosphate is used to make fertilizer.

With all of Africa's valuable resources, it seems the African people would be rich. But the money produced by oil and minerals does not reach most of Africa's people. A large number of Africans live on less than U.S. $1 a day.

High-quality diamonds are used in fine jewelry. Others are used in industry.

Africa's Agriculture

Agriculture is the most important business in Africa. Some people grow food to feed themselves. Others grow plants that they can sell to make money. These plants are called **cash crops**.

Many people in **rural** areas rely on farming to feed their families. They might grow bananas, rice, **maize**, yams, or **cassava**. In many parts of Africa, however, rain may not fall for a long period of time. During these **droughts**, crops die and people go hungry. These **famines** kill thousands of people.

West Africa grows nearly 70 percent of the world's cacao beans. The beans are sold to Europe and North America. Companies turn them into cocoa and other chocolate items. Other African cash crops include peanuts, cotton, coffee, and tea.

More farmers are choosing to grow cash crops. But when too many farmers stop growing food, it leads to food shortages.

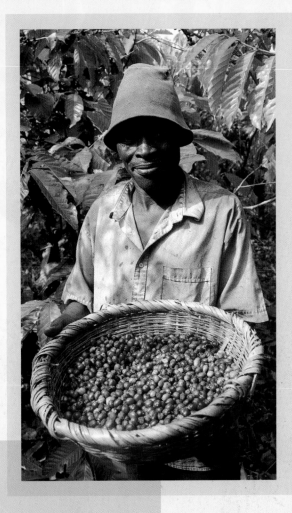

After cacao beans are picked, they are aged, dried, and roasted.

Did you know?

Traders and camel **caravans** cross the desert to get a mineral we take for granted: salt. They load heavy slabs of salt onto their camels. Then they journey for days to reach towns where the salt can be sold.

WHAT COUNTRIES AND CITIES ARE IN AFRICA?

Africa is divided into 54 different countries. Many of the borders between countries were decided on more than 100 years ago. People from Europe, not Africa, created these borders.

Africa's Countries

The countries of Western Sahara, Morocco, Algeria, Tunisia, Libya, and Egypt are sometimes known as North Africa. The other African countries together are called sub-Saharan Africa, because they are located south of the Sahara desert.

This map shows Africa's countries and their capital cities.

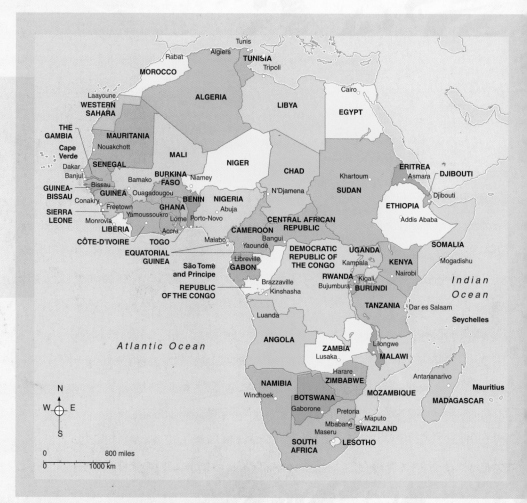

Africa's Colonial Past

In the late 1800s, countries in Europe wanted Africa's land and resources. They divided Africa among themselves. For decades, European countries ruled most of Africa. When one nation controls another one in this way, it is called **colonialism**.

Most African countries did not gain their **independence** until the 1950s and 1960s.

COUNTRY FACTS:

- Largest country: Sudan 967,500 square miles (2,505,813 square kilometers)
- Smallest country: Seychelles 176 square miles (455 square kilometers)
- Largest population: Nigeria 136,769,000 people
- Smallest population: Seychelles 84,000 people

Africa's Cities

About 40 percent of Africa's people live in **urban** areas. Some cities are modern. But many Africans live without running water or electricity. In rural places, only about 1 person in 50 has electric power. Even in some cities, power is not reliable.

Cairo, Egypt's capital, sits on the banks of the Nile River. It is Africa's largest city, with nearly 11 million people. People shop at the city's open-air markets and sip coffee at outdoor cafes. The city's Egyptian Museum displays items from thousands of years of Egypt's history.

Nairobi, the capital of Kenya, is a city of contrasts. Part of the city is modern, with schools, parks, and museums. But more than half of Nairobi's people are poor. Kibera, which is part of Nairobi, is one of the world's largest **slums**. In Kibera, nearly one million people live in metal shacks with dirt floors and no running water.

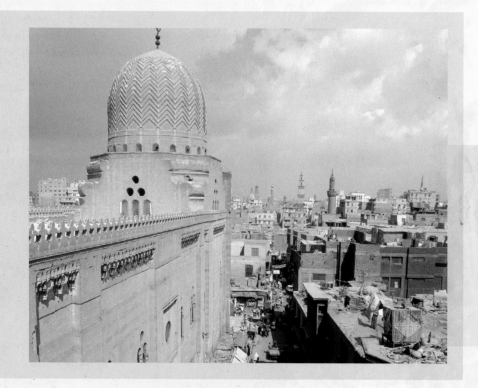

In Cairo, tall, slender towers called minarets rise above the city's **mosques**.

WHO LIVES IN AFRICA?

Africa is a land of many **cultures**. More than 900 million people live in Africa. The continent is home to more than 1,000 **ethnic groups**. People in an ethnic group share a language and a way of life.

More than 1,500 languages are spoken in Africa. But the official language of many African countries is English, French, or Portuguese. This is left over from the days when European countries controlled Africa.

Colonialism brought problems that still exist. Some borders split tribes of people between two or more countries. Others put groups that did not get along with each other into the same country.

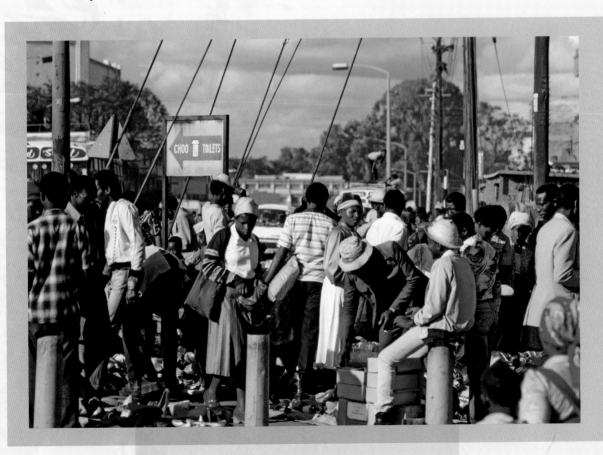

Many Africans live in large cities, such as Nairobi, the capital of Kenya.

Culture and Religion

North of the Sahara, Arabs make up the largest ethnic group. In most of northern Africa, people speak Arabic. The main religion here is Islam. People who practice Islam are known as Muslims.

In sub-Saharan Africa, there are hundreds of different cultures. Kiswahili, Hausa, Fulfude, Yoruba, and Igbo are some languages that are spoken. Many sub-Saharan Africans practice **native** religions. Christianity and Islam are also widespread.

The Tuareg people live in the Sahara Desert. Men wrap their heads in a cloth called a *tagelmust*. This protects them from blowing sand and the harsh desert sun. In the past, Tuareg traders carried goods across the desert on their camels. Some Tuareg people still live this way today, although many have become modern farmers instead.

The Tuareg are sometimes known as the "blue men of the desert." This is because the blue dye from their clothing rubs off on their skin.

The Dogon people live in Mali. Most of them live in a place called Bandiagara, at the base of high sandstone cliffs. Their mud homes and **granaries** blend in with the cliffs that tower above. The Dogon are farmers who grow **millet, sorghum,** onions, and other foods. Tribal members perform masked dances that are an important part of their culture.

The Fulani people live in many west African countries. In the past, as cattle herders, they lived a **nomadic** lifestyle. Many continue to move from place to place to find good **grazing** land for their animals. Others have settled on farms or in cities.

In the Democratic Republic of Congo's rain forest, the Mbuti **Pygmies** live in leaf-covered huts. They gather plants to eat, and hunt small animals with bows, arrows, and nets. They trade meat for aluminum pots, cloth, and grains. They move from place to place in the forest, making new homes with each move. Music and storytelling are important to their culture.

The Dogon people honor the spirits of the dead in a special celebration called a dama.

WHAT FAMOUS PLACES ARE IN AFRICA?

Natural Wonders

Victoria Falls lies on the border between Zambia and Zimbabwe, where the Zambezi River plunges off a steep cliff. When the river is high, the falls are more than one mile (1.6 kilometers) wide.

Kruger National Park in South Africa is a great area for viewing wildlife. Tourists come to see lions, elephants, and many other animals. The animals in the park are protected from hunters.

This map shows where some of Africa's famous landmarks can be found.

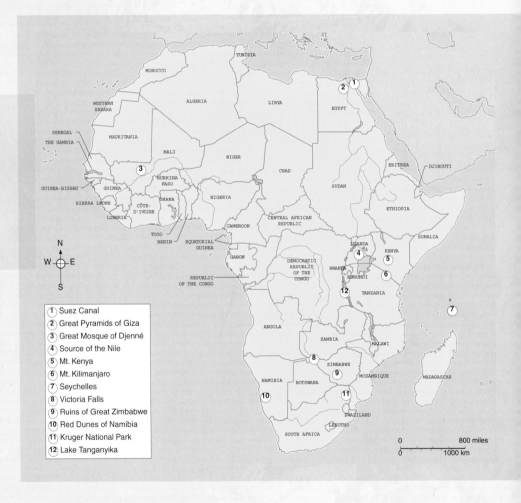

1. Suez Canal
2. Great Pyramids of Giza
3. Great Mosque of Djenné
4. Source of the Nile
5. Mt. Kenya
6. Mt. Kilimanjaro
7. Seychelles
8. Victoria Falls
9. Ruins of Great Zimbabwe
10. Red Dunes of Namibia
11. Kruger National Park
12. Lake Tanganyika

Ancient Remains

Egypt's famous pyramids were built thousands of years ago. The Great Pyramid at Giza, near Cairo, is made of about two million blocks of stone. Scientists believe some of the stones were pulled from 500 miles (800 kilometers) away!

The ruins of Great Zimbabwe are some of sub-Saharan Africa's oldest structures. The city was once home to 12,000 people. It was abandoned more than 500 years ago for unknown reasons.

Modern Landmarks

The Suez Canal in Egypt links the Mediterranean Sea to the Red Sea. Before it was built, ships from Europe had to sail all the way around Africa to reach Asia. The canal, which is 101 miles (163 kilometers) long, was finished in 1869.

The Great Mosque at Djenné in Mali is the largest mud brick building in the world. It was built in 1907 on the site of a mosque from the 1200s. Each year, people climb up the walls to add more mud.

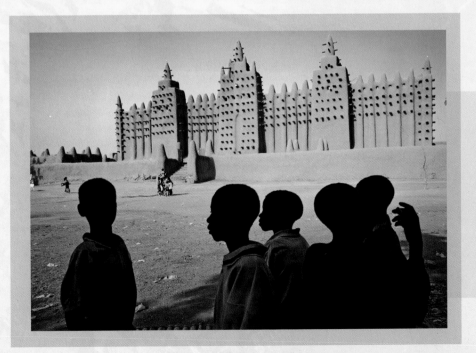

Each spring during a festival, the townspeople work together to prepare more mud to put on the walls of the Great Mosque at Djenné.

27

CONTINENTS COMPARISON CHART

Continent	Area	Population
AFRICA	11,720,000 square miles (30,365,000 square kilometers)	906 million
ANTARCTICA	5,500,000 square miles (14,200,000 square kilometers)	officially none, but about 4,000 people live on the research stations during the summer and over 3,000 people visit as tourists each year. People have lived there for as long as three and a half years at a time.
ASIA	17,226,200 square miles (44,614,000 square kilometers)	almost 4,000 million
AUSTRALIA	2,966,136 square miles (7,713,364 square kilometers)	approximately 20,090,400 (2005 estimate)
EUROPE	4,000,000 square miles (10,400,000 square kilometers)	approximately 727 million (2005 estimate)
NORTH AMERICA	9,355,000 square miles (24,230,000 square kilometers)	approximately 509,915,000 (2005 estimate)
SOUTH AMERICA	6,878,000 square miles (17,814,000 square kilometers)	380 million

Number of Countries	Highest Point	Longest River
54 (includes Western Sahara)	Mount Kilimanjaro, Tanzania — 19,340 feet (5,895 meters)	Nile River — 4,160 miles (6,695 kilometers)
None, but over 23 countries have research stations in Antarctica	Vinson Massif — 16,067 feet (4,897 meters)	Onyx River — 7.5 miles (12 kilometers) **Biggest Ice Shelf** Ross Ice Shelf in western Antarctica — 600 miles (965 kilometers) long.
50	Mount Everest, Tibet and Nepal — 29,035 feet (8,850 meters)	Yangtze River, China — 3,914 miles (6,300 kilometers)
1	Mount Kosciusko — 7,313 feet (2,229 meters)	Murray River — 1,566 miles (2,520 kilometers)
47	Mount Elbrus, Russia — 18,510 feet (5,642 meters)	Volga River — 2,290 miles (3,685 kilometers)
23	Mount McKinley (Denali) in Alaska — 20,320 feet (6,194 meters)	Mississippi/Missouri River System — 3,895 miles (6,270 kilometers)
12	Aconcagua, Argentina — 22,834 feet (6,959 meters)	Amazon River — 4,000 miles (6,400 kilometers)

GLOSSARY

agriculture growing crops and raising livestock

altitude height

antelope type of horned animal that runs quickly

arid dry

border imaginary line separating two geographic areas (like countries)

caravan group traveling together

carnivore animal who eats other animals

cash crop plant grown to be sold for money

cassava plant with a starchy root that can be eaten

colonialism ruling of one country by another

crust Earth's rocky outer shell

culture customs and ideas that a group of people passes on to its children and grandchildren

drought long period with no rainfall

equator imaginary line around the middle of the earth

ethnic group group of people that shares a common culture and history

extinct no longer living or active

famine food shortage

fossil ancient remains of an animal or plant that has been dug from the earth

granary building for storing grain

graze feed on growing grasses or leaves

independence freedom from control by others

landmass large area of land

maize food crop also known as corn

migration group of animals moving from one place to another during a certain season

millet grass that produces small seeds that can be eaten

mineral naturally occurring substance taken from the ground for human use

mosque Muslim place of worship

native to come from or belong to a particular region or area

nomadic moving from place to place

oasis area in a desert where underground wells or springs are close to the surface so plants can grow

peninsula piece of land almost surrounded by water

plateau high, mostly flat area of land

Pygmy member of one of the small-statured peoples of Africa. Some are known as Bushmen or San.

reserves amount of a mineral known to exist but not yet taken out of the land

rural country areas

salt pan area of dry salt where there was once salt water

savanna flat grassland

slum part of a city that is known for its poverty and poor living conditions

sorghum type of grass from which a sweet syrup can be made

urban city areas

FURTHER READING

Ayo, Yvonne. *Eyewitness: Africa*. New York: Dorling Kindersley, 2000.

Bowden, Rob. *Continents of the World (World Almanac Library)*. New York: World Almanac Library, 2006.

The Diagram Group. *African Nations and Leaders (History of Africa series)*. New York: Facts on File, Inc., 2003.

Haskins, James and Benson, Kathleen. *African Beginnings*. New York: HarperCollins, 1998.

Ibazebo, Isimeme. *Exploration into Africa*. New York: Chelsea House, 2000.

Lye, Keith and Porter, Malcolm. *An Illustrated Atlas of Africa*. New York: Zero to Ten, 1999.

Murray, Jocelyn (ed.) *Cultural Atlas of Africa*. New York: Checkmark Books, 1998.

INDEX